Richard Brautigan's Books

Novels:
Trout Fishing in America
A Confederate General from Big Sur
In Watermelon Sugar
The Abortion: an Historical Romance 1966*

Poetry:
The Galilee Hitch-Hiker †
Lay the Marble Tea †
The Octopus Frontier †
All Watched Over by Machines of Loving Grace †
Please Plant This Book
The Pill Versus the Springhill Mine Disaster

*Not Published
†Out of Print

ROMMEL DRIVES ON DEEP INTO EGYPT

ROMMEL
DRIVES ON

Richard Brautigan

DEEP INTO EGYPT

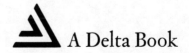 A Delta Book

Some of these poems first appeared in *Poetry, Rolling Stone, San Francisco Express Times, The Free You, Heliotrope Catalogue,* and *The San Francisco Public Library: a Publishing House.*

A DELTA BOOK

Published by Dell Publishing Co., Inc.
750 Third Avenue
New York, N.Y. 10017

Delta ® TM 755118, Dell Publishing Co., Inc.

Reprinted by arrangement with Delacorte Press
A Seymour Lawrence Book
New York, N.Y.

Cover Photographs by Edmund Shea

Manufactured in the United States of America
Second Printing

BOOK DESIGN BY GRABHORN-HOYEM, SAN FRANCISCO

This book is for Roxy and Judy Gordon.

ROMMEL DRIVES ON DEEP INTO EGYPT:

ROMMEL DRIVES ON DEEP INTO EGYPT

ROMMEL DRIVES ON DEEP INTO EGYPT

—*San Francisco Chronicle* Headline
June 26, 1942

Rommel is dead.
His army has joined the quicksand legions
of history where battle is always
a metal echo saluting a rusty shadow.
His tanks are gone.
How's your ass?

A 48-Year-Old Burglar from San Diego

Have You Ever Had a Witch Bloom like a Highway

Have you ever had a witch bloom like a highway
on your mouth? and turn your breathing to her
fancy? like a little car with blue headlights
      passing forever in a dream?

(3)

I remember all those thousands of hours
that I spent in grade school watching the clock,
waiting for recess or lunch or to go home.
　　Waiting: for anything but school.
My teachers could easily have ridden with Jesse James
　　for all the time they stole from me.

Flora Shakespeare

Acting out the place where the flowers die,
circling their graves with themselves,
your costume is perfect, you're on stage.

15%

She tries to get things out of men
that she can't get because she's not
15% prettier.

Romeo and Juliet

If you will die for me,
I will die for you

and our graves will
be like two lovers washing
their clothes together
in a laundromat.

If you will bring the soap,
I will bring the bleach.

Have you ever felt like a wounded cow
halfway between an oven and a pasture?
walking in a trance toward a pregnant
   seventeen-year-old housewife's
   two-day-old cookbook?

Mrs. Myrtle Tate, movie projectionist
died Wednesday in San Francisco.
        She was 66, retired.

We must remember again the absolute
excitement of the moon and think lyrically
        about her death.

It is very important for our Twentieth Century
souls because she was "one of the few women
who worked as a movie projectionist."

Oh, honor this mothersisterbride
of magic lanterns with an endless waterfall of
        visions.

There is something wrong
with this poem. Can you
find it?

Love's Not the Way to Treat a Friend

Love's not the way to treat a friend.
I wouldn't wish that on you. I don't
want to see your eyes forgotten
on a rainy day, lost in the endless purse
    of those who can remember nothing.

Love's not the way to treat a friend.
I don't want to see you end up that way
with your body being poured like wounded
marble into the architecture of those who make
    bridges out of crippled birds.

Love's not the way to treat a friend.
There are so many better things for you
than to see your feelings sold
as magic lanterns to somebody whose body
    casts no light.

The Net Wt. of Winter Is 6.75 Ozs.

The net wt. of winter is 6.75 ozs.
and winter has a regular flavor
with Fluoristan to stop tooth decay.

A month ago I bought a huge tube
of Crest tooth paste and when I put it
in the bathroom, I looked at it
        and said, "Winter."

December 4, 1968

Abalone Curry

I have Christmas dinner every year with Michael
and he always cooks abalone curry. It takes
a long time because it tastes so good and the afternoon
travels pleasantly by in his kitchen that is halfway
    between India and Atlantis.

Cannibal Carpenter

He wants to build you a house
out of your own bones, but
that's where you're living
       any way!
The next time he calls
you answer the telephone with the
sound of your grandmother being
born. It was a twenty-three-hour
labor in 1894. He hangs
       up.

Sheep

Three sheep in a field
grazing beside a FOR SALE sign
are like pennies in the hand
of a child who will buy what
        he wants to.

Donner Party

Forsaken, fucking in the cold,
eating each other, lost, runny noses,
complaining all the time like so
many people that we know.

Formal Portrait

I like to think of Frankenstein as a huge keyhole
and the laboratory as the key that turns the lock
and everything that happens afterward as just the
lock turning.

Everybody wants to go to bed
with everybody else, they're
lined up for blocks, so I'll
go to bed with you. They won't
miss us.

The Sister Cities of Los Alamos, New Mexico, and Hiroshima, Japan

It was snowing hard when we drove
into Los Alamos. There was a clinical feeling
to the town as if every man, woman and child
were a doctor. We shopped at the Safeway
and got a bag of groceries. A toddler
looked like a brain surgeon. He carefully
watched us shop at the exact place where he would
    make his first incision.

Wood

We age in darkness like wood
and watch our phantoms change
        their clothes
of shingles and boards
for a purpose that can only be
        described as wood.

Negative Clank

He'd sell a rat's asshole
to a blindman for a wedding
ring.

Jules Verne Zucchini

Men are walking on the moon today,
planting their footsteps as if they were
zucchini on a dead world
while over 3,000,000 people starve todeath
every year on a living one.

Earth
July 20, 1969

She Sleeps this very Evening in Greenbrook Castle

She sleeps this every evening in Greenbrook Castle
  without the comfort of husband,
and what she knows is what she dreams. He isn't dead
  and he isn't alive,
and the crack of light beneath the door is like the tail
  of a cat as she paces in her room.

She sleeps this very evening in Greenbrook Castle
  without the comfort of husband,
and what she knows is what she dreams. He isn't dead
  and he isn't alive,
and the light in her window is like a wedding ring
  shining to the dark and distant woods.

She sleeps this very evening in Greenbrook Castle
  without the comfort of husband,
and what she knows is what she dreams. He isn't dead
  and he isn't alive,
and the light that reflects her golden hair is the answer
  to her marriage and the children of her prayers.

Third Eye

For Gary Snyder

There is a motorcycle
in New Mexico.

You'll Have to Buy Some More Chairs

If you love a statue start a mirror.
Your friends will admire you.
If you love a mirror start a statue.
Make room for new friends.

Feasting and drinking went on far into the night
but in the end we went home alone to console ourselves
which seems to be what so many things are all about
like the branches of a tree just after the wind
    stops blowing.

Hinged to forgetfulness like a door,
she slowly closed out of sight,
and she was the woman that I loved,
but too many times she slept like
a mechanical deer in my caresses,
and I ached in the metal silence
    of her dreams.

Affectionate Light Bulb

I have a 75 watt, glare free, long life
Harmony House light bulb in my toilet.
I have been living in the same apartment
      for over two years now
and that bulb just keeps burning away.
I believe that it is fond of me.

Just Because

Just because people love your mind,
doesn't mean they have to have your body,
too.

"Butch didn't die in Bolivia. He came
home to Utah—I saw him after he got back.
The Sundance Kid was killed in Bolivia
and it grieved Butch to leave him there."

Wildwood Shadow

He taught me to love him
and called me his flower

An old woman clutches a bagfull of groceries
to her chest. A loaf of white bread sticks
out the top. She has forgotten to put her
food stamps away. They're still in her hand.

Propelled by Portals Whose Only Shame

Propelled by portals whose only shame
is a zeppelin's shadow crossing a field
     of burning bathtubs,
I ask myself: There must be more to life
     than this?

Clad in Garments like a Silver Disease

Clad in garments like a silver disease
you parade around the house. You're quite happy.
The lights are out. The shades are down.
　　It's your own business.

Lions Are Growing like Yellow Roses on the Wind

Lions are growing like yellow roses on the wind
and we turn gracefully in the medieval garden
of their roaring blossoms.
Oh, I want to turn.
Oh, I am turning.
Oh, I have turned.
Thank you.

Nice Ass

There is so much lost
and so much gained in
these words.

Casablanca

Where I come from it's just
another carrot in the patch.
Where do you come from,
stranger?

8 Millimeter (mm)

At the Earliest Dark Answer

At the earliest dark answer
she turns her hair toward
    the door.
She'll learn, she'll learn
that life is more than a
    closing comb.

All Girls Should Have a Poem
For Valerie

All girls should have a poem
written for them even if
we have to turn this God-damn world
upside down to do it.

New Mexico
March 16, 1969

We Stopped at Perfect Days

We stopped at perfect days
and got out of the car.
The wind glanced at her hair.
It was as simple as that.
I turned to say something—

Chosen by Beauty to Be a Handmaiden of the Stars

Chosen by beauty to be a handmaiden of the stars,
she passes like a silver brush
across the lens of a telescope.
She brushes the stars, the galaxies
and the light-years into the order that
    we know them.

Thinking hard about you
I got onto the bus
and paid 30 cents car fare
and asked the driver for
        two transfers
before discovering that I
        was alone.

Please

Do you think of me
as often as I think
of you?

There Is Darkness on Your Lantern

There is darkness on your lantern
and pumpkins in your wind,
and Oh, they clutter up your mind
with their senseless bumping
while your heart is like a sea gull
frozen into a long distance telephone
      call.

I'd like to take the darkness
off your lantern and change the pumpkins
into sky fields of ordered comets
and disconnect the refrigerator telephone
that frightens your heart into standing
      still.

The gunman holds the wind
    in his hand.
Autumn and spring pass like robberies
    across his eyes.
He doesn't blink while one stops leaves
    and the other starts them.
The gunman is a friend to the changing
    of the seasons.
He holds the wind in his hand.

Cellular Coyote

He's howling in the pines
at the edge of your fingerprints.

Parking Omelet

Walking on crow eggs, mama,
listening to the shells break
like cars being parked on
　　asphalt.

Yeah, There Was Always Going to Be a June 5, 1968

My telephone rang in the middle of the night,
but I didn't answer it. It rang and rang
and rang and SHUT UP! and rang as if it were
      possessed.
I always figure that good news doesn't travel
in the middle of the night, so I didn't answer
      the telephone.
I let it go to hell. I was right, too.
It was somebody calling to tell me that Kennedy
      had been hit.

Lemon Lard

Lemon Lard: with your odd snowshoes
and your ability to remember dates,
you're all that you'll ever want to
    be.

Just an ordinary girl, 118
pounds, chipped front tooth, cute,
born in Reno, Nevada, a student
at SF State, she wants candles
married to her womb by the color
of a telescopic saint, so that all
her children will be adventures
    in light.

Fragile, fading 37,
she wears her wedding ring like a trance
and stares straight down at an empty coffee cup
as if she were looking into the mouth of a dead bird.
Dinner is over. Her husband has gone to the toilet.
He will be back soon and then it will be her turn
        to go to the toilet.

It Was Your Idea to Go to Bed with Her

Snowflaked as if by an invisible polar bear
    —unlucky bastard,
you're sitting on the fender of her kisses
while she drives the car down into the
    perfect center of ice.

April 7, 1969

I feel so bad today
that I want to write a poem.
I don't care: any poem, this
poem.

Shellfish

Always spend a penny
as if you were spending a
    dollar
and always spend a dollar
as if you were spending
a wounded eagle and always
spend a wounded eagle as if
you were spending the very
    sky itself.

A Closet Freezes

In a room that knows your death
a closet freezes like a postage stamp.
A coat, a dress is hanging there.

Late Starting Dawn

It's a late starting dawn that breathes my vision,
inhales and exhales the sound of waking birds
and pokes ten miles of cold gray sky at a deer
standing alone in a meadow.

A Witch and a 6 Pack of Double Century Ale

A witch and a 6 pack of Double Century Ale
that's what I want to do on a rainy winter night
at her place.

.

(58)

He wants to fly,
sitting next to me on the bus,
reading a copy of *Flight Handbook*.

He has one of the largest
thumbnails I've ever seen.

As he dreams of bird-like mannerisms,
I stare at his thumb.

Mouths That Kissed in the Hot Ashes of Pompeii

Mouths that kissed
in the hot ashes of Pompeii
    are returning
and eyes that could adore their beloved only
in the fires of Pompeii
    are returning
and locked bodies that squirmed in ecstasy
in the lava of Pompeii
    are returning
and lovers who found their perfect passion
in the death of Pompeii
    are returning,
and they're letting themselves in
again with the names of your sons
and your daughters.

The Elbow of a Dead Duck

A transparent bridge across
the elbow of a dead duck
beckons, friends, like a boiled
    radio station
toward a better understanding
of yourself in these crisis-ridden
    times.

Pretty: except for the
puncture bruises on her
arm. Also, she's a little
thin.

The Alarm-Colored Shadow of a Frightened Ant

The alarm-colored shadow of a frightened ant
wants to make friends with you, learn all about
your childhood, cry together, come live with
you.

Cameo Turret

That's where I
see your face,
baby, on a tank
all around the
cannon.

33-1/3 sized
lions are roaring at the black gates of Fame
with jaws that look like record company courtesans
	brushing their teeth
with would-be rock and roll stars
	in motel bathrooms
with a perfect view of hot car roofs
	in the just-signed-up
		afternoon.

The Virgo Grace of Your Ways Versus This Poem

Hilda,
I keep wanting to write a poem
in praise of your beautiful energy
and because I like the Virgo grace
  of your ways.
Funky as it is: I'm sorry,
forgive me, I guess this is
  that poem.

A Lyrical Want, an Endocrine Gland Fancy

A lyrical want, an endocrine gland fancy,
a telescope that I thought had no thorns
have lead me to a pain that I cannot pronounce.
It gathers around me like a convention of translators
for a language that does not exist with all those meetings
    to attend.

The Moon Versus Us Ever Sleeping Together Again

I sit here, an arch-villain of romance,
thinking about you. Gee, I'm sorry
I made you unhappy, but there was nothing
I could do about it because I have to be free.
Perhaps everything would have been different
if you had stayed at the table or asked me
to go out with you to look at the moon,
instead of getting up and leaving me alone with
     her.

Vampire

Slow/dark . . . black/seeming
approach:
a plant by an open window

January 17

Drinking wine this afternoon
I realize the days are getting
   longer.

Too Many Lifetimes like This One, Right?

Too many lifetimes like this one, right?
Hungover, surrounded by general goofiness,
lonely, can't get it up, I feel just like
   a pile of bleached cat shit.

Color as Beginning

Forget love
I want to die
in your yellow
hair.

In Her Sweetness Where She Folds My Wounds

In her sweetness where she folds my wounds
there is a flower that bees cannot afford.
It is too rich for them and would change
their wings into operas and all their honey
into the lonesome maps of a nonexistent
        California county.
When she has finished folding all my wounds
she puts them away in a dresser where the
drawers smell like the ghost of a bicycle.
Afterwards I rage at her: demanding that her
affections always be constant to my questions.

Up against the Ivory Tower

I'm sitting here (at a cafe) thinking
about writing a poem. What will I write
about? I don't know. I just feel like it
when suddenly a young man in a hurry
walks up to me and says, "Can I use your
       pen?"
There's an envelope in his hand. "I want
to address this." He takes my pen
and addresses the envelope. He's very serious
about it. He's really using the
       pen.

All Secrets of Past Tense Have Just Come My Way

All secrets of past tense have just come my way,
but I still don't know what I'm going to do
next.

Melting Ice Cream at the Edge of Your Final Thought

Oh well, call it a
    life.

My Concern for Your Tomato Plants

I stare at your tomato plants.
You're not, I'm not pleased with the way
        they are growing.
I try to think of ways to help them.
I study them. What do I know about tomatoes?
        "Perhaps some nitrate," I suggest.
But I don't know anything and now I've taken
to gossiping about them. I'm as shameless
        as their lack of growing.

Pity the Morning Light That Refuses to Wait for Dawn

Pity the morning light that refuses to wait for dawn
and rushes foolishly with its mercury pride to challenge
a responsibility that knows only triumph and gently bends
the stars to fit its will and cleans up afterwards all
that poor wasted light, leaving not a trace behind.

Snow Makes Me Sad

Flying East today first to Chicago,
then North Carolina snow makes me sad
below in the mountains of the West.
It is a white sadness that rises
from California, Nevada, Utah
and Colorado to visit the airplane,
to sit here beside me like a snowy 1943
    map of my childhood.

As the Bruises Fade, the Lightning Aches

As the bruises fade, the lightning aches.
Last week, making love, you bit me.
Now the blue and dark have gone
and yellow bruises grow toward pale daffodils,
then paler to become until my body
is all my own and what that ever got me.

I Am Summoned by a Door

I am summoned by a door
but forgotten by the knock
and left standing here alone
in a long silent hall, like
a marble intestine, that knows
my name.

At Last Our Bodies Coincide

At last our bodies coincide.
I'll bet you thought this
would never happen. Neither
did I. It's a pleasant
surprise.

Let us please learn new words that mean as much as direction:

Let us please learn new words that mean as much as direction: wife.

Deer Tracks

Beautiful, sobbing, high-geared fucking
and then to lie silently like deer tracks
in the freshly-fallen snow beside the one
you love. That's all.